Songs of a Sistermom

Motherhood Poems

To Sistermom Allison,

Thank you for supporting my art! Enjoy these songs from the Sistermom in me to you. May they inspire your continued motherhood journey!

With Love,

Soror Charisse
&
Sistermom   6/2004

Songs of a Sistermom

Motherhood Poems

Charisse Carney-Nunes

Brand Nu Words

Published by Brand Nu Words
The literary & performance division of Nunes Productions, LLC

1314 Fairmont Street NW
Washington, DC 20009
www.BrandNuWords.com

ISBN: 0-9748142-0-2

Library of Congress Number: 2003099507

First Edition: March 2004
Printed in the United States of America

Dedication

*First giving honor and glory to God, and to
Jesus Christ who is my Savior.*

*For the wonderful women who have inspired me over the
past four years – the Sistermoms.*

*Sistermoms, Inc. is dedicated to supporting and enriching the lives of
African-American mothers and their families. Knowing these women
and the commonality of our struggles has enriched the fiber of my
being. Whether it's the challenge of working through that "NAPPY"
hair, maintaining a positive outlook on love and life, balancing the
demands of work and family, or losing and finding yourself again as an
individual, my "sister" moms provide support, inspiration and love.
And so I dedicate these songs to them, as without them I'm not sure I'd
have had the courage to sing.*

Contents

THE NINTH SYMPHONY

Foreword

It is a rare pleasure to closely observe the birth of someone else's long-time dream. Usually, we are so involved in our daily lives that it can be difficult to make the spiritual and emotional space to embrace the dreams of others. Fortunately, Sistermoms has enabled me to open my life and heart to some very powerful African-American mothers, and to share their dreams – not only for themselves, but also for their children and families.

Sistermoms, Inc. grew out of a deep-seated, personal need of my own. As a mother of two young children, one of the things I lacked in my life was a strong network of women whom I could trust with my most closely-held thoughts, dreams and fears – those issues that I struggled with in the middle of the night: am I doing the right thing by working full-time outside the home; is my son developing into a strong, respect worthy young man; is my daughter nourished and seeing the range of role models that she needs; how overweight am I getting; how is my relationship with my husband; where can I find a great babysitter/school/dance class/cleaning service? The list goes on, and the answers are uniquely based upon one's own cultural experience.

Growing up, I was blessed to have a mother who surrounded herself with a circle of women whom she loved, shared and trusted with her life. As a new mother, I yearned for this support. Although I knew many people, lived in the city in which I was raised, and had a career that connected me with lots of knowledgeable people, most of my friends lived elsewhere, were single or did not have children. We were simply living very different lives.

I needed my own network, and as a professional recruiter I had the skills to develop it. So I turned to our pediatrician for help. She had built a huge practice – very diverse –

and was well respected throughout our community. Also, as an African-American mother, she could relate to my situation. She knew many other women facing the same challenges. She also knew the importance of creating a "village" for yourself and your children. So, she talked to the moms of some of her other patients. She gave them my number, and talked about what we were trying to create. And women called me. We talked, we shared, we laughed, and even shed tears of disbelief at the commonality of our struggle. We met, and in November of 1999, Sistermoms was born. Since then we have grown into a close-knit group of 30 and an Internet community of more than 120 African- American mothers.

So what is a Sistermom? The definition continues to evolve. A Sistermom is an African-American mother who understands that motherhood is a rare and special gift, and that enjoying the journey means not losing yourself in the process. It means creating the kinds of supportive networks – the village that you and your children need not only to survive, but also to thrive healthily and happily in this very challenging world. For those moms yearning for this reality or for those who need to expand their village – there is Sistermoms.

Through this (r)evolutionary process, I met and became friends with Charisse, a wise, amazingly powerful woman with tremendous talent, as you are about to learn. Sharing her poetic voice is one of her long-time dreams, and it became mine too as a result of our involvement in Sistermoms. Charisse is a rare and special woman, and I am sure that after reading this book, your own world will be changed, even just a bit. As you enjoy these "songs" of this very special "Sister" mom, I welcome you to add a word into your vocabulary: Sistermom!

Linda Henderson Burke
"Head Sistermom"

At last
My love has come along
My lonely days are over
And life is like a song.[1]

PRELUDE
TO THE DANCE

THE ETERNAL LOVE SONG: A DUET

I loved you...
When God reached down and shaped you in his image
When He took a part of you and made it me
When He placed the stars above the earth and heavens
When He lit the sun to burn eternally

I loved you...
When God took my bones and flesh and made it you
When He first gave the gift of life and then of love
When He gave me such a soul so I could love you
When He gave colors to the rainbows up above

I loved you...
When my womb became the birthplace of the Old World
When my breast provided nourishment for all
Where I, too, was once known as a worthy warrior,
        as a scholar and a queen,
Yes, I stood tall

I loved you...
When the valleys of the Nile served as our lovebeds
When I built pyramids from water and from sand
When I fathered every part of Ethiopia
When I ruled with you as King of all the lands

I loved you
When the strangers stole our bodies out of Eden
When my sisters died upon the ocean floor
When all I knew was stench from blood and death and misery
When nothing you could do,
Would heal my ailing sores

4

I loved you…
When a floating dungeon was our only castle
When we were packed like cargo riding on the waves
To a place that never understood our royalty,
To a place where we would only be enslaved

I loved you…
When I kissed your bloody back so I could heal it
When you'd almost lost your hope and all your drive
When the cotton fields of then served as our lovebeds
When I dreamed for you,
To keep your soul alive

I loved you…
When I reached for you through darkness bound by
shackles
When my comfort and my love were the only key
When you were beaten and then forced
              to bear their children
When my songs of hope and praise kept your spirit free

I loved you…
When your strength and your direction led us through it,
Through the dark and dreary days that were our past,
Through the struggle and the hatred soon to follow,
You were by my side undertaking every task

I loved you…
When your dedication built our bridge to freedom
Away from all those dreary years of death and strife
Your peaceful love unlocked a nation's conscious
Your strength gave us a passageway to life

And so my love I've known your soul forever
Though we've just met we've loved since time begun
And now I know I'll love you for forever
Today our spirits dance to life's eternal song
Yes, today our spirits dance to love's eternal song!

WE HAVE OUR LOVE

Just as a dancer has her music
We have our love

Just as a singer has a melody
We have our love

Just as the meadows have grass, flowers and spacious air
We have our love.

Just as a bird has song
>   A poetess . . . her poetry
>   A mother . . . her child
>   A goddess . . . her beauty
>   A passion . . . its fire

We have our love.

As long as God's earth gives us air to breathe . . .
I will love you.

THE MIRROR

When I look at you
I see myself

Someone full of love,
       hopes,
       dreams,
       aspirations.

Someone full of compassion,
       caring,
       honesty,
       temperance,
       and love.

Someone who loves too hard,
       falls too hard
       unafraid to admit
       with will and strength
         to love hard
           and hurt hard again.

You
Helped me wipe away the foggy steam
And when I looked inside . . .
       there was only one of us.

And somewhere
       in that mirror

I found you
And we found my life,
       your life
         our love.

I KNOW

When I was a little girl
When life was easy
When things were simple
When daddy knew everything

I remember thinking . . .
       but how will I know?

Well now I'm not a little girl
And sometimes life ain't easy
And things are often complicated
And I've learned that no one knows everything

I still sometimes think . . .
       how will I know?

But when he makes life a little easier
And when he makes love seem so simple
And when you love each other though neither of you
know everything

You start to rest assured . . .

My life
My love
My friend
My best best friend
And finally . . .
You know . . .
You just know.

CAPTURE

When love tries to capture you
    It's like a mystical and magical mirage
    It's like falling through a gentle summer breeze
    It's like sailing through the sands of God's creation
    It's like replacing the impossible with ease.

When love tries to capture you
    It's like a violent storm that will not end
    It's like a sea of passion and of fire
    It burns out of control of all mankind
    It's like Kilimanjaro -- only higher.

When love tries to capture you
    It blinds you with the beauty of its light
    And sometimes with its fervor it brings fear
    It's like the wildest beast of God that must be tamed
    But once you own it you will always keep it near.

When love tries to capture you
    Even if you are determined not to listen
    You'll hear so clear the knocking at your door
    And when love comes in your prayers will all be
    answered
    For God has sent you harmony and love forevermore.

When love tries to capture you
When love tries to capture you
When love tries to capture you

Just let ... it ... in.

A MOTHER'S LOVE LETTER

Dear Son-In-Law,

A mother's love is unconditional
A mother's love is pure
A mother's love has no shame
A mother's love is forgiving
A mother's love is patient
A mother's love is kind
A mother's love is a true gift from God.

"As you join with my child today . . .
you must love her as I do . . .
>*unconditionally*
>*with pureness of heart*
>*without shame.*
>*You must keep forgiveness in your heart*
>*(and use it when it is necessary).*
>*Be patient and kind*
>*and always keep God at the center of your selves*

For if you love my child as I do . . .
Then I will love you as my child."

> Love,

> Mom

WHY I'M MARRYING YOU . . .

Because . . .

Love is life
Though life is sometimes dark
But dark gives way to light
And light brings forth the Sun
And the Sun brightens life
As you have brightened my life
And so you are my life
And so, too, you are my love.

MY HAVEN

When I think about the love we share
It makes me warm inside
It makes me feel all snuggly
It fills me up with pride...

To know, that I have you...
To love me
To live me
To breathe
To feel me
To fill me
With all that you are ...

That's what makes me warm
That's what makes me all snuggly
That's what makes me so content
And keeps me safe...
In the place you made for me,
Yes, just for me...

Safe within that inner part of you
That place
That sanctuary
That Shangri-la
That you built within your being
That place that I will never leave
My heaven, my haven, my love.

WEDDING DAY HAIKU

Time springs eternal
Love's swallowed me whole – my heart
Nestled in your soul.

Unsure of what the balance held
I touched my belly overwhelmed
By what I had been chosen to perform. [2]

HYMNS OF
PREPARATION

THE CHILD YOU'LL BE

I think about the life you'll live
The dreams you'll dream
The love you'll give

I think about the air you'll breathe
The songs you'll sing
Sorrows you will grieve

I think about the stars you'll reach
Even the books you'll read
And the goals you'll seek

I think about the child inside
My heart and soul
And I confide

Inside myself
There's nothing more
That I can see
Except to dream
And think about...
The child you'll be.

DON'T QUESTION A BLESSING

I've got battles to fight
Wrongs to right
Fancies to flight
And even riots to incite
But my grandmamma said, "Don't question a blessing."

I've got bills to pay
Mountains in my way
Majestic paths to survey
And mighty plans to obey
But my grandmamma said, "Don't question a blessing."

I've got mistakes to clean up
A life to construct
Outlined impervious strategies
Too pristine to disrupt
But my grandmamma said, "Don't question a blessing."
So divine intervention
Done hijacked my vision
Stole my definition
Of purpose and mission
Made off with my plans
And thieved my demands
On my future defined
And entrenched in my mind
And entrenched in my mind
And entrenched in my mind
But, damn, who am I?
Just a vessel for proof

of God's undying truth
and faith undenied
as life forms inside…

'Cause my grandmamma said, "Don't question a
blessing."

Progeny's Poem of Haiku

You exist in me
Then emerge like August sun
Taste life's milk from me

SWAN SONG

They think…
Your soul was but
      An angel's kiss
      A willow's wisp
      A dew drop's misty
            brief existence on a meadow's morn

But,
You were BORN
Within the depths and definition
Of all that I knew I had been
      Thought I was then
          And all that I dared to dream I'd be

See,
You were BORN
Long before the beginning when you were conceived
Long before the initiation of your flesh in me
Long before the commencement of your growth received
Attention
From those to whom I dared to mention
The dawn of your existence in mine
And in time
I came to know
The essence of your burgeoning soul
As you thrived I felt you grow
Until the whole
      of your existence became mine

Time, I thought was on our side
Yet God sent your spirit on a ride
Deceived all notions of idyllic time

Still, I know

Your existence in me
    Was evidence of the miracle of life
    The essentiality of faith
    And the permanence of everlasting love

My little lost love…
May God send His angels from above
    To carry your enduring soul

Nestled safely within her breast and wing
Sing, forever my little love,
Sing.

CONTAINMENT

You entered my life
Through the colors of my imagination
Dancing, whirling, spinning
Through every cavern
of my mind
And through the fire and salty oceans of eternal love for
him
You entered our world
I
a mere vessel
Unable to contain
The erupting exaltation
That is you

Emergent Love:
My Thoughts By the Ocean

Your love,
Intricate
Moved me like the whirl of the wind
      Moved sand into dunes.
Enveloped me like
      breaking waves storm onto the waiting shore.

As sure,
      as I had ever been, I knew
your love,
      it
          drew
             me
                in…
with the force of the fierce and awesome undertow

I came to know
      your love…
an untamed ocean
      yet you
          quintessence of devotion.
You made me love you
As you made loving me
      your first
          your best priority
Loving me so sensually
Entering my heart through my soul
Eternally
How could I know
That I could ever love you more
Until the core
Of everything we are

23

Changed one night and
Emerged like morning star
      into
            our
                  room.

Through shadows, daunting fears and gloom

Exposed
My womb
Exposed.

But you were there with me
      in
            that
                  room.
You were there
When spinal needles penetrated me
Like broken beached glass and sand stuck in a little child's
shoe

When fear enveloped me
Like broken waves upon the shore

And I was sure

With every push, every push

As I bore down our lives
Into one
So same
So young
Yet replete with vibrant promise of
Tomorrow yet to come

I was sure
That because
You were there
     in
         the
             room
Emerging from my womb
There
A safe space
To create
Fate

And vibrant promises of a forever
     Of our tomorrows.

WITH GOD'S WILL

In the midst of
My joy with you
My eyes reflect the
Flickering glow
Of candlelight
My nose
Takes in scented wick and wax
Coalesced with
Rawness of
You
And
Me
My fingers wipe the
Brow of perspiration
As thoughts race of
Naked aspirations
Of what could be
What should be
What just might be-
come of our love
making: Our hearts and minds
Grasp possibilities
That too often elude
Yet remain ever-present
Coalesced with
The candle
The aroma
The perspiration
Alas: a glistening tear of
Aspiration
Makes its way

Out of our collective ducts
And down my
Shivering cheek

LIFE AS LIMERICK

There was a young woman from Tuscan
Whose figure was svelte, stacked and buxom
    But then 10 months ago
    Her tummy started to grow
And her hubby then refrained from lusting

So the young woman took to the hills
Where she met a new suitor named Bill
    Bill loved both baby and mom
    In his infinite charm
And bought her full-figured nighties with frills

But we're never gonna survive
unless we get a little crazy. [3]

FROM
B FLAT TO F SHARP

GOT MILK? GIVE LIFE.

Breastfeed your child
      In the bathroom
Breastfeed your child
      In the backyard
Breastfeed your child
      In the dining room
Breastfeed your child
      In the den
Breastfeed your child
      In the bedroom
Breastfeed your child
      In the basement
Breastfeed your child
        Anywhere on God's green land
           That you
               Can.
On the bus
On a boat
On a train
And definitely breastfeed your child on a plane
      With both of you a little closer to heaven

In the center of the center rush hour subway car
Breastfeed your child
At the grocery
At the Car-mart, Walmart and K-mart
Breastfeed your child
And definitely breastfeed your child at Targét
Breastfeed that baby at the rest stop on the highway
Windows down

Breastfeed your child

During conversations with whoever about
whatever whenever and wherever
Breastfeed your child at Thanksgiving Dinner in between
the cornbread stuffing, collard greens, and macaroni and
cheese
Please
Breastfeed your child on Christmas morn
video camera on
recording faithful dawn

On the corner or in the middle of your block
Breastfeed your child
At the post office
At the park
At a party with the lights dim or glaring mid-afternoon
glow
Know
You MUST breastfeed your child
Where you worship
In between prayers for forgiveness, remembrance,
and reverence of thee
You see

Anywhere on God's green land
That you
Can.
Got milk?
Give
Life

NAPPY

Little girl…
Our hair is…

    …super-napturally NAPPY
    …super-abundantly NAPPY
    …super-eminently NAPPY

    Our hair is…
    "break the comb" NAPPY
    …"run out the chair" NAPPY
    …"scalp just caint bear" NAPPY

    Our hair is…
    …"left-hand turn" NAPPY
    …"scream for a perm" NAPPY
    …"perm 'til you burn" NAPPY

    Our hair is…

Pull	ouch
Twist	ouch
Turn	ouch
Kink	ouch
Coil	ouch
Snap	ouch
Crack	ouch
Pop	ouch
NAPPY!!	

But girl, God didn't give us nothin' we couldn't handle.

    It's "back of the bus" NAPPY
    It's "Underground Railroad" NAPPY
    "Ain't I a Woman" NAPPY
    "Lay down with Massa" NAPPY
    And bear his children NAPPY

Though misbegotten NAPPY
While pickin' cotton NAPPY...

Our hair is...
>Harriet Tubman
>Sojourner Truth
>Mary McCleod
>Rosa Parks
>Ella Baker
>Josephine Baker
>Zora Neal Hurston
>Ida B. Wells
>Sonja Sanchez and
>Angela Davis...
... NAPPY

'Cause girl,
God didn't give us nothin' that we couldn't handle.

I Used To Be a Poet

I used to be a poet
>Words flowed so freely heart to pen
>Soul soared as high as nature's wind
>Deepest thoughts were my best friend
>Consecration was my yen

Ooooo yeah, I used to be a poet

I used be a lover ... yeah, that's right, a swingin' single
>My love would have my men transfixed
>Passion was fierce and kept us gripped
>Love made us quiver like eager lips
>Ooooo, and the way I moved my hips!

Oh yeah, I used to be a lover

I used to be a revolutionary ...
>"Power to the people..."
>That was the call I'd loudly herald
>My blood and fire could not be quelled
>Thought men today could change this world

Ooooo yeah, I used to be a revolutionary

Then, I became a mom

Unabashedly, solely, exclusively, singularly, and entirely a mom
>Just like my milk flowed on demand
>I'd give my soul with one command
>Blindly thought poop and pee were grand
>Chaos that few would understand

Ooooo yeah, exclusively a mom

But then, in between that 2 A.M. 4 A.M. 5 A.M.
screeeeeeaaaammmmming
Between that 5th 6th 7th 8th – okay 12th dirty diaper that I
changed
In between those precious eyes, behind that fervent smile,
and just beyond her nature's glow
Realization! The single most poetic, passionate,
revolutionary thing I could ever know
Was to cultivate up the warriors of tomorrow.

So, I'm still a revolutionary
      But with wisdom as my pearl
      I know tomorrow's boys & girls
      Dwell endlessly to change our world
      Still a revolutionary

And, I'm still a lover
      But now her love has me transfixed
      On those precious eyes and lips
      Her dawning soul just keeps me gripped
      Still a lover

And, I know I'm still a poet
      God granted me what is my yen
      Her love inspires my heart to pen
      Our souls soar higher than the winds
Ooooo yeah, I know I'm still a poet.

CHRISTMAS EYES

Look into my eyes
Tell me what you see…

    The joy of good tidings
    The pureness of light
    A reason for living
    The miracle of Christ

    The radiance of moonlight
    The bliss of the sun
    The promise of tomorrow
    For a life just begun

    Timeless beauty of evergreen
    The infinity of the wreath
    The stillness of peace
    And the gentleness of sleep

    The valiance of faith
    And strength from above
    The exuberance of laughter
    The reverence of love

Look into my eyes…
It's Christmas

LEROY'S SONG

the teacher said
that little leroy did it.
"that's okay," she told his mama
"boys at this age sometimes touch;
it doesn't mean very much – of anything."

so mama went home.

but at the parent teacher conference,
those words made mama cringe...
"mrs. jones, little leroy did it, again."
"don't worry,
        boys this age they think they're tough
sometimes on the playground they like to play rough
it was an accident, but...
    i just wanted you to know that little leroy did it.

so mama went home.

but then the very next tuesday, it happened again
mama wanted to jump out of her skin
again. the teacher said, "little leroy did it."
work left out
"leroy did it."
runs and shouts
"leroy did it."
used his outside voice when in
in fact, he just wouldn't listen
that voice was just too loud
said he teased the other kids with his proud proud ...
                                    ways

"but don't worry, sis
i just put him on a list
for 'special' ones
those who might just have too much fun

37

or keep a substitute on the run
don't worry, mom, and don't go home fussin'
like i told you before, it's nothing!"
"but know this, little leroy did it."

so, mama went home.

and so it went for years and years
mama ignoring those nagging fears
overlooking neglected tears
and so it went for years and years
and each time she knew, her little leroy did it.

and by the 10th grade
        they'd thought they'd had it made
but the principal called her in
to tell her it had happened again
"mrs. jones, leroy did it."
distracting all the other students
"his behavior simply isn't prudent
but don't worry, did we forget to mention
boys like 'this' sometimes just can't pay attention?"
so they gave him a pill.
so what, they said, you don't think he's ill
still, this will still him 'til he will sit still
        enough to learn.
don't worry mama, GO HOME.

so mama went home.

so by the 12th grade
armed with all this knowledge
leroy knew far too much for anyone's college
and anyway what was the use
his future was murdered, his dreams in a noose
and he knew
she knew
they knew

i knew
we knew
hell, even you knew
all too … well
no need to dwell and dwell
just tell…
us what we already knew
"leroy did it."

mary sue had been defiled
"leroy did it."
mr. greenberg had a missing child
"leroy did it."
cars been thieved for miles and miles
"leroy did it."
hell, if james brown ever lost his style
we would all know that "LEROY DID IT!"

so after leroy's graduation
no need for all the adulation
no need for all the celebration
no need for college invitation
no need for white man's education
frustration.
castration.
damnation
causation?
no one knew.
but that leroy did it, they'd always know
so, leroy and mama …went home.

postlude:
eenie meenie minee mo
catch a nigga manchild by his toe
if his mama don't holla, won't let him go
eenie meenie minee mo

COMPREHENDING MADNESS

Andrea Yates killed her babies
Now, I'm not talkin' 'bout just a little bit of killing
I mean one, two, three, four, five of God's little angels …
dead
After loving and trusting, done been misled
From the sanctuary of mother's womb
Down the dead end path of a porcelain tomb.

Andrea Yates done killed them boys
…and baby girl, did she enjoy?
Chased 'em round and round 'til she overpowered
One by one
Life is done
Life's done
Within an hour
False demons … now … devoured

The nerve to claim her mind had snapped!
Thought them dirty little angels just needed a bath
…in the cleansing blood of Jesus last …
          embrace.

If she was really tryin' to make them immortal,
Why'd she leave one floating in vomit, blood, and water?
Hmmm
Andrea Yates just KILLED them babies.

Poor Mrs. Yates
Motherhood too much to bear
Full of disappointing dark despair
Left her gasping for constricting air
Drowning in unanswered prayers
…on life she'd entered unprepared.

Did she really think we'd understand?
Damn…
Andrea Yates killed them babies.
Do you really think that she went crazy?
Maybe…
She was just too damn lazy
For the sleepless, endless
     Boundless
         Thankless
             Sometimes could care less
                   Job of motherhood.
But shhhhhhhhhhhhhh
I ask you now for thought and food
How many of Us understood
that mood that threatened and sometimes could
drag us to the dark side of motherhood?
And like Andrea, we think we never would.
Silent shame
How many of us
(even a little bit)
Understood?

41

YESTERDAY YOU KISSED ME

Yesterday you kissed me...
    And the
    Whole of my soul opened up like a bottomless
cavern
    My mind unable to fathom
    How the brush and the touch
    Of your lips against mine
    Could move me so much

Yesterday you kissed me...
    And my
    Eyes became intoxicated with the beauty of your
ginger-kissed skin
    Then, drawn in
    My ears inebriated with the sound of your laugh
    As my nose rose
        to become under the influence
            of the congruence of the aroma
                of your candy-like essence
                and the scent of your
            quintessential innocent core

So much more...
You are
All that I have ever wanted
But more than I could have ever conceived
You to be

You are
My hope for tomorrow
My evidence of the permanence of love
My confirmation of the supremacy of my Creator from
above

And though I have loved
     you from the birth of our eternity on Earth
Yesterday, when you kissed me
     The reality of our duality and
     The infancy of our legacy
     Permeated my comprehension
     Of who
        I
            Am.

HARD HEADED

I'll tell you a secret
If you don't tell a soul
Don't want no one to know
How I'm losing control…

    My little girl…
    …is hard-headed.

Hard-headed, I say
With no doubt with chagrin
She's got that angelic face
But that devilish grin

    See, my little girl is just hard-headed.

She's no little girl lost
And yes, sometimes she'll listen
Still she does things her own way
Under any condition

    Well, my little girl is just hard-headed.

I say head … she says heart
I say stop … she says start
I say up … she says down
I see sunbeams … she just frowns
I say sleep … she stays awake
When I say to give, it's her cue to take
"Quiet please!" … compels mighty screams
She'll force mere bystanders to their knees

And with herself, she's mighty pleased
As one day, I will too be glad
For independent will and strength iron-clad
But for now, dear Lord, save me from going mad

'Cause my little girl, is just hard-headed.

A Sonnet for Mabel

Screen door crashed open
Ma's booming voice and piercing eyes
Crying and groping
Searching for sense in midst of lies.

Sirens still ringing:
"Damn you, release my child."
Jackals start singing
Normal's gone wild.

"Brand new '63 Chevy?
For what? My son has no use!"
Arms flail, chest was heavy
Her robe's knot came a loose.

"Mrs. Johnson, here cover your breast."
But she spat on his badge, for love of her crest.

HAIKU FOR MY GIRL

Rambunctiously bliss-
ful of spring's bursting blooms. You
Mirror my spirit.

HAIKU FOR MY LITTLE MAN

Unflaggingly play-
ful of autumn's new growth. You
Compel me toward peace.

Because the greatest love of all
Is happening to me
I found the greatest love of all
Inside of me. [4]

THE NINTH

SYMPHONY

UNLEARNING THE LESSONS OF LIFE

Some say, "Older, wiser
We grow,
The more we live
The more we know."

But with chaos confusion
Stress and strife,
Me...
I'm tryin' to **UNLEARN** the lessons of life.

Forget the daily
Race race race
Forget my ignorance of
Time and space.

Forget my tendency
To never slow
Or to rush right past you
If you say, "hello."

Forget my pessimistic
Oversights
Or my incessant cursing
At a traffic light.

Forget the way I've felt
When torn apart
And the tears and frustration
Brought by a broken heart.

Forget my dwelling
On my failure last
And my stark unwillingness

To forget the past.

And my inability
To just "let it go"
Forget these lessons and…
I'll *really* grow!

And when I **UNLEARN** the lessons of my life
I'll quiet my heart, my mind,
 my soul to hear…

> *Miss Sue (clap clap); Miss Sue (clap
> clap). Miss Sue from Alabama, she's
> givin' a party!! A boom chick-a-boom-
> chick-a-boom-boom-boom*

To hear the happiness, harmony, inner peace inside
Voices of love, contentment — my child inside.

For when we **UNLEARN** the lessons of our lives
Only then, yes then, can we revive
Revive that inner child inside.

LIFE

Life...
    Is such a splendid thing

When your eyes see all the joys it brings
When you let love allow your heart to sing
Yes, life ... is such a splendid thing

And even if the path you take
Is vast and long and makes you wait
Before revealing all you anticipate

Life ... is such a splendid thing

The thirst for knowledge was the dream
Illusive as it sometimes seemed
Yet when the quest for love remains supreme
Then passion now equates your dreams

And, life ... is such a splendid thing

NATURE'S KNOWLEDGE

A rose knows
to hold
steadfast to the whole
of the Earth,
soaking in the nourishment
of God's fire and rain.
Don't disturb
or you might get burned,
        or cut,
                or scratched.
Yes, a rose knows
to hold
steadfast to the whole
of the Earth.

So, I approach
and try to drink
        the wisdom of the rose
                through – my – nose.
Therapeutic medicine
        for melancholy mood.
Quick fix
        guarding against
                quest to control –
                        everything.

Now, like the rose,
I know
to hold
steadfast to the whole
of the Earth,
while we can.
For every season shall cease some time.

So, as this one ends,
I approach my friend again.
And pull him out of the Earth.
And through my eyes
I drink in the wisdom and the beauty
of his petals blowing in the wind.

Asanté

Asanté
Asanté
Asanté
Asanté Sana
Words my ancestors used
To Honor
The dear departed dwellers of the Kingdom
From decades before them

And I
Descend from them
And use
Asanté Sana
To honor the spirit of the living souls
Dwelling within my own…

Asanté to the spirit of Jesus the Savior
        For it is He who inspires my aspired behavior

Asanté to the spirit of my beautiful mother
        For her grace and compassion inspire my love
for…
                        my child.

Asanté to my father; though his spirit may not be affective
        It's profound and has taught me both faith and
perspective

Asanté to a sister's undying devotion
        …a divine first example of pure love and emotion

And to that pedophile "grand"father … that sex slayer of
souls

      Your contradictions compelled my resilience and growth

Asanté to my brother
    My aunts
          My uncles
           My cousins
Your multiplicity of being provides life's lessons by the dozens
Asanté to every wise woman who I call "friend"
Asanté to my loves lost like whispers in the wind
      For without you I'd have never learned to love myself within
And to my husband who completes me in ways I've just begun to comprehend
And to my child and those to come with love to endlessly descend…
Asanté
Asanté
Asanté

SOUL MATE SONG

The very first time that he kissed me I knew...
He ... was my soul mate

Soul because it was the whole
      Of his spiritual existence that penetrated mine and
Mate because it could have been none other than fate
      That could create
      The state
      Of this duality

And when my soul ... mate ...
      Suggested that the essence
      Of this spiritual duality
      Emerge into one from two
      I, too, knew, that a lifetime ago or two
      Our former souls had already wed
      So yes, I said
      I do

I do . . .
      Love you
      Live you
      Think you
      Drink of only you

And I knew . . .
      That I would love him till mortality tears us apart
        . . . but between you and me,
        after 10 years of "bliss" in our hearts . . .

I've decided, in my next life . . .
      I'm coming back as a lesbian!

CELEBRATING SILENCE

When
Did life become a clanging cymbal?
A noisy gong?

What was once a symphony of
you and I
morphed into cacophony
MommyDaddyMommyDaddyMommyDaddy
MommyDaddy
life?

Palms wet and blood-splotched red from pressure
over my ears.
My head, will it explode?
Stop!
The noise that we've become,
today.

Still,
we've danced a thousand dances,
kissed a thousand kisses,
and tried a thousand times.

Though, the symphony is gone…

if we climb
into remaining
quiet of our minds.
To replay the dances,
to dream of the kisses
to imagine a thousand new ways
for us to dance, to kiss, to love, again.

Embracing love,
someplace very silent,
we can travel
to the quiet of our minds
cast aside the
MommyDaddyMommyDaddyMommyDaddy
MommyDaddy
talk.

A moment in time
to dance anew
kiss anew
ignite anew the flicker that was our fire.

Sweet silence, hear it whisper,
"It is there,

within
that very quiet someplace —
within the quiet of our minds."

MOTHERHOOD MOVEMENT

Have you heard, have you heard, have you heard, have
you heard
      have you heard…
            of the Motherhood Movement?

Mothers moving all over this earth.
      Reclaiming those who they birthed.
          Reclaiming all that's their due.
              Doing, thinking, feeling, moving,
                  whether by thousands
                    by hundreds
                      by dozens or
        twos.
They are reclaiming their due.

Can you feel, can you feel, can you feel, can you feel, can
you feel, can you feel,
      the motherhood storm?
          Marching upon you with the force of a
      trumpeter's horn.

From New York, where Amadou Diallo's bullet torn
                      spirit won't
          rest…
To New Guinea, watch police slay Steven, Peter, Thomas,
      Matthew and freedom
      for non-violent protest.

Mothers cross oceans avenge senseless death.

From the Congo where rebels steal 7-year old angels on the
      run,

force them to choose 'tween death or donning
guns...
To Connecticut, where cops stopped somebody's child by
mistake,
and after brutalizing his head, and his groin, and
his face,
and exposing his nakedness in virtual rape,
Hartford police claim in denial he
can't make a case.

Mothers are forging a dignity race
(for our lives).

From Burundi where unarmed women, children and even
babies have been shot,
as millions close their eyes or callously watch...
To Bosnia where thousands of war criminals reign free,
despite known rapes, vast genocide, and crimes
against humanity.

Mothers now march to end world insanity.

From Rwanda where the world watched one million
Africans die,
and sits silently today as murderers laugh at those
crimes...
To Richmond where homosexuals heed prophesy of
unsolved homicides,
and Henry Northington's headless spirit eternally
cries.

Evil rejoices, paradoxically beguiled,
But mothers will rise up combating the vile
Every soul on this planet is somebody's
child

From Chicago to Chechen,
From Baltimore to Biloxi,
From Canada to Cambodia,
From Kenya to Kansas,
 Every soul on this planet is somebody's child.

From Portland to Paris,
From Indiana to India,
From Ecuador to El Salvador,
From St. Louis to St. Petersburg,
 Every soul on this planet is somebody's child.

From Texas to Tiananmen,
From Switzerland to Swaziland,
From South Africa to Southern California,
From Austria to Australia,
 Every soul on this planet is somebody's child.

From Kyoto to Korea,
From Kuwait to Quatar,
From Cuba to Costa Rica,
From Algeria to Alabama,
 Every soul on this planet is somebody's child.

And who if not MOTHERS
 save a world gone defiled,
  than the one who gave life to
 unappreciative child
   after child running rampant
  disrespecting her earth...
Yet she maintains compassion for all who she birthed.
And through wretched barbarity she still sees our worth
While she diligently marches us on toward rebirth...

Reminds us as we sin with her eyes open wide
Every soul on this planet is somebody's child
Every soul on this planet is somebody's
child.

Have you heard, have you heard, have you heard, have
you heard
have you heard...
of the Motherhood Movement?

WE WOMEN

With our kind gentle ways, and a smile on our face...
We women, will change the world.

With effervescent commitment, yet little resentment...
We women, will change the world.

Though our backs may be tired,
                  we still somehow rise up...
We women, will change the world.

Though we seldom get credit, no matter who says it...
We women, will change the world.

So we just keep on going, at work and at home and...
We women, will change the world.

When there's problems at home,
                  it ain't right in our soul 'til...
We women, will change the world.

And we put ourselves last,
                  'til those problems have passed...
We women, will change the world.

Yes, we just cannot rest, 'til the world's at its best so...
We women, will change the world.

Through the anguish and pain,
                  that our womanhood brings...
We women, will change the world.

And we know humor and laughter, cures any disaster…
We women, will change the world.

And our dreams and our goals,
                            are entrenched in our souls…
We women, will change the world.

And our daughters we'll teach,
                            as we practice and preach…
We women, will change the world.

And tomorrow, we say, will outshine today . . .
We women, will change the world.

With the courage & sanity,
                            to have birthed God's humanity…
We women, will change the world.

And with temperance of mind, and the wisdom of time…
We women, will change the world.

Yes, God gave us humility, yet every ability so…
We women,
        yes us,
                we women
                    will change the world!

SHAKE WHAT YOUR MAMA GAVE YOU

Shake what your mama gave you
Shake what your mama gave you
   I said
   Shake - what - she – gave
   You girl
   Vision to rule this world
   She gave you
     truth
   Just like a newborn baby
     Maybe just maybe
   Mama knew
   Trials you'd be going through
   Dreams that would go askew
   Gave you hope set to birth anew
   Armed she-warrior debut
   All that you have to do…
   Is
Shake what your mama gave you
Shake what your mama gave you
   She gave - what - she – gave to shake
   It's not yours to desecrate
   Not for profane remakes
   Not Alex O'Neil-like fake
   Her legacy, don't forsake
   No, child go and make
   Her proud
   Sing your songs of realness loud
   Real loud
   Tales of devilish dragon disavowed
   When you
Shake what your mama gave you
Shake what your mama gave you
   So you shake what your ma bestowed

Freedom like Rita Dove
Secret power like DaVinci code
Chart of less traveled road
Legends of truths untold
Langston's sagged heavy load

Shake what your mama gave you
Shake what your mama gave you
Shake what your mama gave you

Or it *will* explode.

ACKNOWLEDGMENTS

*Thank you to my husband for giving me the vision
and courage to give myself the permission to take the
time to write these songs.*

*Thank you to my editor, Darrell Stover, my proof readers,
Virginia Lazala and Henry Carney, my partner and guide,
Mirian Torain, my publishing associates, Kwame Alexander,
Carole "Ife" Keene, and Laura Daye, as well as my entire circle
of friends and family who took the time to help my words fulfill
their destiny to live and dance eternal.*

ABOUT THE AUTHOR

Charisse Carney-Nunes, freelance writer and attorney, is a proud alumna of Lincoln University in Pennsylvania – the nation's oldest historically Black college, where she was the Poet Laureate of the University for two years. She is also a graduate of Harvard University's JFK School of Government and the Harvard Law School. The birth of Charisse's daughter in 1999 provided her passage to her writing renaissance. Since that time, three of her works have been published, including a short story and poem in an anthology entitled the HIP HOP TREE, and a poem, entitled "Nature's Knowledge," in the literary journal, EARTH STORIES. Charisse is currently co-authoring two books tentatively entitled, "The Christian Family's Guide to Celebrating Kwanzaa" and "Sistermom Speak."

The 1999 birth of her daughter also led her to the motherhood support circle, Sistermoms, Inc. Charisse is a co-founder of Sistermoms, an organization that supports African-American mothers and their families. These amazing women have compelled Charisse's growth as a mother, a wife, an author, and a woman. Charisse resides in Washington, DC with her husband of eight years and her daughter.